Black Gardenias

A Collection of Poems, Stories & Sayings from a
Woman's Heart

D1613521

Antoinette Karleen Ellis-Williams
Foreword by reg. e. gaines

Black Gardenias: A Collection of Poems, Stories, and Sayings From a Woman's Heart

Copyright © 2013 by Antoinette Karleen Ellis-Williams
First Printing March 2014

Published by Semaj Publishing

Edited by Yasmine Christian

Photo by Leona Strassberg Steiner

ISBN: 978 0-9772572-8-7

Library of Congress Control Number: 2014933045

This book is available at a special discounts for churches, schools, and other educational institutions.
Contact Semaj Publishing
201-500-4066

Author Bookings and Management
semajpub@hotmail.com

Dedication

Black Gardenias is dedicated to all the women bold enough to live their lives with dignity in the face of pain brought on by structures of: oppression, sexism, racism, and classism. Despite these forces of oppression this book highlights the ability to stand, move forward, sit, but always to survive.

It is also for the millions of black women who went to their grave with a secret they were unable to share with another sister. *Black Gardenias* is for all the many unarmed women murdered in America like Renisha McBride, Kendra James, Rekiba Boyd and for Marrissa Alexander standing her ground. This book is for my students who have shared their secrets and stories with me. They have inspired me, trusted me and humbled me. This book is for my grandmother Gladys Mae Ashley Wint, who taught me to laugh with grace, to live an authentic life. She was the most beautiful woman I have ever known. I dedicate this book to my mother, Marlene Yvonne Ellis, who taught me how to keep secrets with her own stalwart approach to life, always able to tunnel through dark places no matter what. My mother is the bravest woman I have ever known. This book is dedicated to my father, Beresford Ellis for teaching me how to cook and season food. His heart is bigger than our pots and more flavorful than any spice. I am grateful for the love he instilled in me for sharing, hospitality and faith in God.

I dedicate *Black Gardenias* to my husband Junius W. Williams, for loving me, warts and all. He has encouraged me to focus my passion and complete this work. Thank you for always making me laugh. Finally, to my sons Junius and Che', you have both made me truly understand love and opened my heart in unimaginable ways.

Acknowledgements

Thank you to all my friends who have stood by me in good and bad times. I am deeply humbled and honored to have reg. e. gaines contributing the foreword for this book. His body of work as a spoken word artist, poet, playwright, and advocate brings a critical voice and validation to this work. He gets it!

Special thanks to Sheila Kirven, Brenda Brown, Sharon Graddy, Minister Renee Johnson and Gail Maynor for patiently listening to my poems from time to time. Thank you Bill Lee for your guidance in this project. I love you, Ben Jones for encouraging me to use my art to create change. Very special thanks to Dr. Eddie Glaude, Angela Burt-Murray, Cazzie Pantoja, Dr. Faith Samples-Smart, Darnell Moore, Nicole Miller, Dr. Linda Epps, and Tynesha McHarris for taking time to read and review this book. I also want to thank artists Stephen B. Ellis for his graphite pencil drawing *Shades of Me*, Sidney Wilfredo King III and Paul el Sadate for their generosity, each piece beautifully illustrates the words and verse of the text.

I want to thank LaVon Featherstone and the entire Semaj Publishing family for their patience, enthusiasm, assistance and support with this project. Your care, compassion and professionalism provided a rich environment for the completion and success of Black Gardenias, my first book.

I want to acknowledge my colleagues in Women's and Gender Studies and the sisters of Yemeya of the Black Administrators Alumni, Faculty, Staff and Student Organization (B.A.A.F.S.S.O.) at New Jersey City University.

Finally to my pastor Rev. Dr. William Howard for his wisdom and unwavering support with this book and helping me to understand the liberating Gospel of the free Jesus. I love my church family Bethany Baptist Church in Newark, New Jersey; you have blessed me in so many ways, thank you for your unconditional love.

Table of Contents

Introduction   *9*

Foreword   *13*

History & Heritage

    Yellow Daisies   *17*

    My Grandmother Never Ate Grits   *21*

Mothering/Children/Elders

    Gloved Doves   *23*

    Mama's Lessons   *24*

    Play, Play   *26*

    Chocolate Baby, Sweet Honey Bee   *26*

    Letter From Mama Olewagi   *27*

    Speak for me Mama   *31*

Abuse & Identity

    Faded Wildflowers   *33*

    Nikki Devon---Pale Blue Shades   *62*

    Identity Crisis   *65*

    Cleaning Woman's Left Foot   *67*

    Sticks and Stones   *68*

Body, Love, Sex and Men

    To My Afrikkkan Brothers   *71*

    Baby Sue's Sonnet   *75*

    Rebe's Regret   *77*

    Pretty in Pink   *79*

Little Miss Perfect   82

Spring break is broken Friday the 13th 2009 84

Friendship & Sisterhood

Shanay Shafequka Tamia Watkins   89

Market Women -All is Well   93

Friends By and By   95

Sister Mother-less, Mother   96

Time Stands Still, My Friend   98

Sister Friends in My Head   99
(Jill Scott, India Arie, Michelle O.)

Faith & Church

Church Time   102

Purple Felt Hats   104

Adhan, A Call to Prayer   107

Sunday Morning Rain   108

The Source of Our Strength   109

Justice

Lilies in the Fields   111

Saturday Night Round Up   113

Guilty Found Innocent/Innocent Guilty   114

The D is Silent   116

Epilogue   119

Introduction

Black Gardenias is a collection of poems, short stories and sayings whispered by women; ancient and present who have loved, conquered, danced, prayed, struggled, overcome, suffered and laughed. It is about how women love and laugh in spite of hardships. Some of the women in this collection reflect on rape, incest, and abortion. Others share their joys and pains of childbirth, sex, God, marriage, and love. Still others discuss resistance and politics, beauty and femininity. *Black Gardenias* for me is a collage of Black women, which transcends time and place, fluid and powerful. A testimony of our ability to connect and disconnect with our most constant force— God.

"The gardenia is a beautiful flower, takes a lot of work to grow. However, if you can grow it, this flower is a very beautiful flower... says, 'You are lovely' and it is even a symbol **of a secret love."** (http://en.canadianflowerdelivery.com/flower-meaning/gardenia.aspx)

According to Jennifer Bourn, "Black is associated with power, fear, mystery, strength, authority, elegance, formality, death, evil, aggression, authority, rebellion, and sophistication. Black is required for all other colors to have depth and variation of hue."

Black Gardenias explores the history and heritage of Black women, the pleasures and pain of mothering, and nurturing our beautiful children. Just like the title of this book, Black communities have had tremendous obstacles to face, yet they have produced brilliant flowers, e.g. "The rose that grew from concrete" (Tupac, 2007).

Sometimes we fill our aching soul with prayers and hymns, remembering stories of slave catchers, branding irons, human cargo, Klansmen's whips, crooked bosses, nasty teachers who touched us in math class, or cheating lovers; remembering the loss of our innocence or a stolen love affair; or our medical diagnosis these are all part of our Black woman narrative. Stories bring women together and remind us of what it means to be woman in a culture that hates women and an African encased in blackness surrounded by whiteness.

This book will explore issues of abuse and identity, hidden from public view. We all have secrets never spoken but they are always present. Secrets that we dare not utter out loud because of the shame they may bring to us, or our people. These secrets are omnipresent hanging thick in the air as the humid summer's day. We hope to mute their guttural hollas, and whimpering songs with laughter or silence. They are always there. But secrets are not always bad; they are the private dreams, wishes, and possibilities we cherish in a place locked by our own egotistical mind and selfish desires. They are forever hidden giving pleasant relief, memories from mundane reality. They are our friends, the soundtrack we download bopping our heads to their mysterious seductive beats.

In this book you will meet several women, like Frances, Rebe, Baby Sue, Nikki, Devon and Mama Olewagi, who want other women to never forget to pass down history, traditions and sometimes secrets to girls burgeoning to womanhood and women afraid to live. Some of these women who want to escape and other women want love and still other women are just doing the best they can. Women who are bold and fight for justice in the face of injustice. *Black Gardenias* represents the collective memory of voices, stories, pain, laughter and triumphs that Black women share while sewing together threads of unwavering perseverance that unite all of their voices.

Black Gardenias is similarly about the journey a black girl takes to womanhood and aging, finding her distinctive placement in family with the expectations of culture to represent "us". The journey at times is one of necessary isolation but never alone or loneliness. Traveling with the weight of collective expectations and experiences, at times dampers the personal *I/me* voice. We hear these voices pushing up and through the concrete pavement of essentialism and constructive regressive narratives of the "should be" and "should do".

Throughout this book you will see quotes from men and women who recall things their mothers told them. These recollections serve as memory crawls, "Mama notes" to our life song.

This book is for people who understand the power of telling stories and speaking truth. Men will get a glimpse behind our cultural veil and historical shroud. Perhaps the poems will permit you the opportunity to understand and renew the journey of mutual respect and solidarity. This book is for every woman and poet to hear the rhythmic beat of ancient struggle and resistance. This is for men who love women, women who love women and people working for justice. It is for the hip-hop artists, educated scholars, people of faith, those looking for something to believe in and those from the school of life. Read this in barbershops, beauty salons, college classrooms, cafes, and on your front porch.

Foreword

Antoinette Ellis-Williams', Black Gardenias, is a rich, lush literary journey which conjures images of Black Women, their struggles, their loves, their lives. Her keen sense of legacy connects the reader with historical artifacts drawing us in close proximity to unprecedented times of hardships. The difficult moments when Black Women were and, to a large degree are, forced to play foundation to an entire race's climb from deception and despair. Ellis-Williams wordplay is but one of the many surprisingly fresh takes on the genre. That she also fuses essay, with poem, poem with dedication, supplies her with a more than unusually large canvas with which to stroke, brush and paint her formidable ideas. That the genres collide then collapse, spilling effortlessly into one another, allows us unprecedented emotional access to the lyricism and musicality of her poetry. Space, taut line breaks, the relentless infusion of cinematic shot lists drench us in colors, structures, sounds and smells. We are not readers but instantly listeners to the text, where moments of jazz like silences allow one to look inward, at what part we have played in the construction of Ellis-Williams poetic confessions. Like a brilliant painting, conceived after years of experimentation, when abstract expression crashes head first with improvisation, the tones and shades, the many contradictions, are both simple and complex. I merely need to think of the poems, Pretty in Pink, or Guilty Found Innocent/ Innocent/ Guilty, to remind myself why Ellis-Williams' words are so necessary. Brilliant poetry usually begins with brilliant titles. The ambiguity, allowing readers freedom to imagine, is equivalent to a musical hook. One would be hard pressed in today's world to hear/ see the word pink and, to some degree, literally be forced to have images of Breast Cancer Awareness. This is neither ambiguous or new. But from the first line, we are submerged in a tale, personal and introspective yet, universal in scope and theme. If Trayvon Martin is not a name you know, Mars must be the world in which you inhabit. Ellis-Williams' connection between the many fallen Black Males at the hands of those who protect and serve, juxtaposed with a Black Woman's sensitive but accurate depiction of how we are all Trayvon, but also, all guilty, speaks to the power of poetry. Life is lost every day for the lack of poetry in our lives. Antoinette Ellis-Williams' Black Gardenia's helps to fill that void and is a must read, sure to make minds question, and hearts bleed.

reg e gaines
Tony Award/ Grammy Award Nominated Playwright, Poet and Author

Black Gardenias

A Collection of Poems, Stories & Sayings from
a Woman's Heart

Antoinette Karleen Ellis-Williams
Foreword by reg. e. gaines

Yellow Daisies Oil in Canvas
by Antoinette Ellis-Williams

HISTORY & HERITAGE

Yellow Daisies

I
Standing in cotton and tobacco covered fields
Piles picked and bundled here and there,
Brown dusty shacks in the distance
80 or 96 graves with wooden crosses line Potter's hill
But we knew every man, baby and woman that rests in those
Wooden graves
Abe, Shango, Lester, Lulu, Mama, Judifer, John, Alma,
Venette, Sarah, Buster Ray, Cody and
Countless others
Buried beneath sweet peppermint, basil and thyme
Herbs that are used every day
Nothing went to waste and always
Found a way to nourish us in life and death
Lives sometimes filled with pain from whips,
Axes from slave catchers' blades, and even suicide
Lives occasionally filled with laughter from babies
toddling, and loving
In fields of wheat, singing of redemption
And of home in Ghana
Reached the Promised Land and
In returned sent us precious herds
Sweet and savory like their courage and love

II
Over yonder on this day
Fine dignified beautiful men in kingly gingham blue
cotton shirts and
Pretty strong, delicate, elegant women finely clothed in
print and plaid dresses.

17

Thick plaits, locks, matching tie heads and ribbons
Elegantly placed on wooly crowns
Pleats neatly ironed and starched
Covered welts, burns, bruises and soars
From hard dirty work, ugly dehumanizing work

III
Parson Anderson journeys to Peterson's plantations to
Lead the regular soul saving ceremony of the heathens
Unusual activity is heard on this day in distant shacks
Dancing music, rejoicing songs
Old home tributes proudly echo through
The fields
African drum beats
Funga, Afro Cuban and Calypso beats
Are new to the white preacher's ears
Parson Anderson believes the service has begun
But his heart grows fearful of the power of the drum
Ancestral drums, and chants grow louder
The African Holy Spirit is already present and strong
Without his dry sermon of damnation
And destruction.
Parson Anderson is paralyzed, confused
And afraid.

IV
Sister waves a new broom
Specially woven for Sister Miaha's day
She dances down the field,
Waving the broom and singing, "Sister's getting married!
Sister's getting married!"

Beautiful brown skinned Miaha wears a new
White cotton dress and wide brim hat with a red silk
ribbon made by Sister
Yellow daises are gently held in her hands to

Complement her wedding dress

V
Mister Jude Wilson her betrothed is fine in his
Black coat and white starched shirt
His top hat crown him for the most
Special of occasions

Parson Anderson knows this ain't no regular
Soul saving service
He hollers to stop the drumming, stop the dancing
Put away the broom

VI
Today this celebration will not be crushed with screams
of heathen
African sinners and lake of hell fire.
The African Holy Spirit is too
Much to conquer
Nanna Olajah
Leads the ceremony
Paterson and Parson Anderson
Fall to their knees and drop their guns and Bible,
Recognizing the power of the Truth
And the power of the people

VIII
Sister sings
Miaha smiles and grasps her yellow daisies
Mister Jude proudly holds her hand, he says
*"I promise to love honor and protect you and
keep only to you. In sickness and in health."*
She says,
*"Take this ring and wear it and think of me every day and
every hour. You will know that my heart and yours are
one. And after I'm dead and gone to live in the fields of*

herds, yellow daises will grow to let the world know that I always loved you."

Nanna Olajah instructs the couple,
"Jump the broom and kiss your bride."

My Grandmother Never Ate Grits
(Excerpt from manuscript When the Curry The Grits)

My grandmother never ate grits
She never sang freedom songs nor lived
In the Jim Crow south

My grandmother was black
As tar, sturdy as a mango tree planted by the Caribbean
Sea
Her hands were calloused from
Washing clothes against zinc washboards with blue soap
Her feet were hard from walking without
Shoes early on in life
She walked straight and tall
From carrying water pails on her head
From the stream miles from home

My grandmother never
Ate chitterlings or smothered chicken
Her pots were lined with
Cornmeal porridge, lobster from the sea,
Callao and salt fish
Bammy and dumplings

Her clothes were made from her Singer machine
She cleaned for white people and washed their clothes
My grandmother never ate grits

But my grandmother's arms kept me safe
From the duppies
Her songs of *Jane and Louisa will soon come home*
Soothed my fears away
Her black cake made Christmas the best
Soaked in wine and white rum
She never ate grits but

Carried a cutlass like the warrior woman
Nanny of the Maroons
To kill chickens for dinner, fight intruders
And kill any beast seeking to prey
Upon her brood

She was mother and father
When parents had to leave
And go to work
She was the voice of God
When she taught us how to say our grace
She never ate grits
But was like all other grandmothers from
The motherland's shore
Strong, loving and present
        At every turn

"And you shall teach them to your sons, talking of them
when you sit in your house and when you walk along the
road and when you lie down and when your rise up."
Deut. 11:19

MOTHERING/CHILDREN/ELDERS

Gloved Doves

honey hibiscuses, red azaleas line
forest green verandas
elegant perched doves sit on swings
sipping Aunt Lucy's limeade.
Buicks, Cadillacs and tricycles
go by
gloved hands wave to neighbors
and say
hello.
Wingspan across the block sheltering
Sick, lonely, tired in the flock
Gloved doves chirp and sing.

"Always do your best, the angels can't do any better."
John Hope Franklin, Historian

Mama's Lessons

For the times she combed my hair/pulling and tugging, I
yelled and cried.
I learned to sit still.
For the times as a young girl, she allowed me to crawl in
her bed when the storms were raging outside. The safest
place in the house was nestled next to her.
I learned that storms would pass.
For the times she wiped fever from my brow and fed me
bush tea.
I learned to honor the land.
For all the secrets I told her, to only her.
Her non-judgmental ears just listened and laughed as I
whisper about kisses from men.
I learned to whisper secrets to few select friends.
She often said, "My child, we have a choice, we can
either cry or laugh." She laughed through most of the
ugly things and the pain.
I learned to laugh through my trials.
For always telling me not to hold anger, hurt or pain in
my heart.
I learned to let go.
For showing me how to care for my babies.
*I learned to hold on to my sons and that I must let go of
them, if they are to walk.*
 For showing me how to make rice and peas and stirring
butter and sugar the right way so the black cake would be
smooth.
I learned to cook with loving patience and soul.
For warning me that marriage has bitter and sweet but
always make the sweet outweigh the bitter.
I learned to love my man.
For asking nothing from me except to past her sweater
from time to time.
I have learned to give to my elders.

For helping me to stand up straight.
I learned to walk with dignity and pride.
For telling me that girls should close their legs when they sit.
I learned to respect my body.
For loving me unconditionally.
I learned to love myself.

Play Play

One-Two-Three-Four Five
Daddy thinks that I'm so nice
Six-Seven-Eight-Night-Ten
He tells me I am his little spice
      Sugar, Sugar, Sweet as can be
      Sugar Sugar, sing to me
Jump in the middle
Jump in the hat
Jump over Bobby's black Tom cat
One-Two-Three-Four-Five
And that is where my story's at.

Chocolate Baby, Sweet Honey Bee (dedicated to JuJu and Che)

Chocolate baby
Naked boy,
Chocolate baby
Running through the street
Sweet potato bunny
Sweet as can be
Chocolate baby
Naked as can be
Sweet potato bunny
Jumping in the bed, falls on my foot
And bumps his head
They are my cuties, yes indeed
Chocolate baby and my
Sweet honeybee.

"You can't stop playing the piano until you are sixteen."
Virginia P., Newark, New Jersey

Letter from Mama Olewagi

My dear daughter,

Today my arthritis is not so bad so I thought I would write you this letter. Imagine that I am still able to write some words on a paper and almost ninety years old. I keep following those spirits. When the spirit says move I move.

Remember growing up in Khamasi. I can still hear your great grandmother humming as she hung out the clothes to dry, cousin Zambi playing with other children from our village. "ZZ jump, ZZ skip, ZZ play with an old chew stick." Funny I can even remember me crying because ZZ kept teasing me because my feet were bigger than other nine-year-old girls and very ashy. "Ola, Ola big foot gal. Steps on the cat imagine that." Those were good days. The air was fresh and I knew all my neighbors for miles. There were many days I left you with ZZ's mother or with Momma Ya's mother. And I never worried about anything. I never had to carry food or clothes for you or your brother. We all ate out the same pot. Peanut stew was your favorite. Your little black eyes would smile at me each time you saw the peanuts and fish stew.

Remembering these things is easy. I can't even remember what happened yesterday or who came to see me. When did I see you last? I have 10 or is it 12 tablets I have to take every day, blue, pink, green and black, red, and white. I keep telling them give me some cassava porridge and ginger tea with some hot pepper, two lemons, green bush, some eucalyptus rub and little castor oil. They think I am some crazy voodoo priestess. They don't respect scared things, ancestor's treatments, and prayers, songs and stories. They just keep giving me these pills. Well darling daughter, I stopped taking them two weeks ago. I hide them under my tongue and just smile. Then I spit them in the trash. I have already begun to feel so much better. My stomach stopped hurting. Much better.

At ninety I should know my own mind. Nothing's wrong with my mind just my legs gone. My dear Ife, Sitting in this wheelchair hurts my soul. My mind is still out in the village running after you and your brother. I am still flexible and nimble. But then I see a glimpse of myself in the closet mirror, I am afraid. Afraid I don't know who that old woman is staring back at me. She is a stranger to me. Her wrinkled fragile bruised body feels uncomfortable. My thick plaits are now gone. Even my teeth are gone. It's this American food and water polluting my body. But I know the good Lord still with me. He is a good God. Even if everybody left me.

Ife, I have lived a good life, a full life. I have watched friends and family die, cars, trains and buses pass by, I have seen planes and computers all in my life. But I never thought that you and your brother would have put me in a place like this. A nursing home, a place with unloved and sick old strangers from a different land. No Africans my age here; just some young rude selfish girls. Some of them are from Nigeria, Uganda and Gambia. But they care for me like I am a stranger. But I am their Momma, their Auntie. They have no time to hear my stories. I know you are busy with your family and your travel plans. You have your own health problems I know. I know that your diabetes is affecting your eyes. But my own grandchildren hardly visit me. Never would know that I have 10 grandbabies. But they lives all busy too-- Teachers, lawyers, doctors, administrators, construction workers, mothers, musicians, and artists. These are my babies, my blood, and my legacy.

Daughter dear, I don't want you feel no ways bad but I have always told you my mind. A white American nursing home is not home. I want to go home to my Africa soil and die. I need to see the Gold Coast once more time before I leave this place. I want to taste peanut stew and pepper pot soup. Not like the kind in America but the kind Momma Ya made. The sun has to touch my gray skin.

I am weary and all alone in this place. You have to let me go. I have to be free. I am caged up in this place. The smell of sickness and death is everywhere. I need to go home. Please Ife take me home. If you love me set me free. I will watch over you wherever I go. Just let me go to the land that I know. My mother and father are there. All of our people are there. Now it's time for me to go.

You have been my joy, now it's time to say good-bye. If you don't take me home I will set myself free.
Your Loving Mother

(Originally Published in <u>Temba Tupu!: Walking Naked, Africana Women's Poetic Self-Portrait</u>, Edited by Nagueyalti Warren, African World Press, Inc., 2008.)

"Surely goodness and mercy shall follow me all the days, all the days of my life. And I shall dwell in the house of the Lord. And I shall dwell in the house of the Lord. Surely goodness and mercy shall follow me all the days, all the days, of my life."

"Some glad morning when this life is over, I'll fly away. To a home on God's celestial shore I'll fly away... when this life is over I'll fly away."

Speak for me Mama (Inspired by the Essences 2001 Image Awards)

I choose you to be my mama
Safe in your womb, warm and dark
Away from the bright lights just
Warm inside you
Your heart makes me dance and
Rocks me to sleep
Nestled in your womb.

Doctors say I won't survive the journey
SIDS they fear, birth defects, low birth weight
Speak for me mama/ tell them I'm fine
Warm in your womb
Mama please go to the doctor, take your vitamins
Put down the pipe and bottle
They say if I make it to my first birthday
I may not survive the lead paint in our building
Or rats that run around
Speak for me mama/ kill the rats for me
Make them paint the apartment
Speak for me mama/ please
They say that the drugs, guns and violence are too much
For me to live
Speak for me mama/
I was here before, your son
I was going to be a doctor or a preacher
Remember? I was the one that was killed in the drive by
Remember? I am the one who died of an asthma attack
on the
Cold school bathroom floor
We were the four little girls who died in Sunday School
by a bomb
Of hate. Remember? I was the one you threw off the ship
to save me from a life

31

Of bondage, whips, shame and pain. Speak for me mama/
Remember? I was the one beaten and bitten by Bull
Conyers dogs and police.
I was the one lynched by the Klan. Robert Moss was my
name.
Bill Holliday sang me a song, *Strange Fruit* she called
me.
Fight for me mama
Resist for me mama
Better cops, better schools, better health care, better food
Cook me steamed salmon, kale and broccoli sometimes
Warm in your womb away from the cold bright lights
Speak for me mama/ so I can live
Warm, safe, nestled next to you
Early cold graves are lonely/ so
Speak for me mama/ your baby in your womb.

ABUSE & IDENTITY

Faded Wildflowers

I remember the day so clearly. The smell of Aunt Freda's cornbread and catfish pudding fills the air from the old coal iron stove. Mama's husky Southern voice echoes from the kitchen as she sings songs of Jesus' redemption and cuts mustards, collards and cabbage. *"What a friend we have in Jesus all our sins and grieves to bear."* The scent of stale Jean Nate perfume is mixed with Uncle Palmer's Camel cigarettes and whiskey as the juke joint folks sit on the porch and tell stories of Granddaddy. The day began as so many others before but ended like no other since.

Sarah Jane Banks and Addie Mae Franklin, play aunties from up the way, can be seen walking up the hill in their tight flowered print dresses, pointy shoes and bright red lipstick. Mama use to call them "the no class hussies". "Dem ain't no kind of proper ladies, always cussing and whoring around. Never seen so much red in all my day!" Calling Mama judgmental was an understatement.

I discovered what she meant by "proper" when I met Marva Whitman in graduate school. Marva swore she had breeding but she was rough around the edges, maybe that's what I liked about her. She was a hustler, not the obvious rough neck kind of hustler but the sort that's smooth, like fine bourbon or hot chocolate over ice cream—sinfully delicious. After leaving Cleveland, she received a scholarship to Smith College in Massachusetts where she majored in Women's Studies and Political Science.

Marva was the one who taught me the word lesbian when I first went to New England twenty-five years ago. Never knew they had their own proper word for what I saw all my life until I went to live with white people in the north. Can you imagine their own word for; well you know what I mean? Aunt Sarah and her friend Miss Ade

Mae lived together for nearly 40 years. Daddy always told us that they were a "funny" kind of women. I just thought they liked to laugh a lot when I was a kid. What did I know? Who knew that this "funny" thing was about who you slept with? They seemed like they never made any trouble they just laughed, worked and loved. Aunt Sarah sad now 'cause her friend, Miss Ade Mae, died last year in a peaceful sleep. She just went to sleep and never woke up. That's the way to go if you ask me.

I just don't see all the fuss about who you love. 'Ain't nobody's business! As for Marva Whitman she was tough on me. I know I should talk nice 'bout everybody. Granddaddy use to tell me, "Frances don't nobody like the truth." He told me that lying is what people really like, especially church folks. "Frances, imagine if you told dem ladies that dey hat was downright ugly, or dat de choir was off key or dat you sick of dat usher's auxiliary man, Brother Lippman selling candy for some bus ride to the same old place again." He would say, "Child, you can't let folks know what's in your mind. It's 'bout survival. Your words can choke you if you not careful. The truth is nobody can stand the honest sure nuff raw truth."

I sure miss him. He was like a worn musty blanket, a little itchy but always warm. He smelt of tobacco and sweat. The dirt under his fingernails and his tough callused hands always made his hands appear dirty. As a little girl I use to hate the feel of his rough scratchy hands on my skin. It felt like sandpaper against my smooth dark skin. But the strange thing now is that I would give anything to feel Granddaddy's callused dirty hands against my face.

Granddaddy worked for at least 12 to 16 hours seven days a week in the fields. I would help him prepare the earth or just watched him plow when I was a little girl. He would say, "Dirt is holy, its clean work, a man need to work to have dignity. If he ain't got work where's his dignity?" I wonder what he would have to say about the unemployment rate of young Black men today? Granddaddy was my Stokely Carmichael, Huey P. Newton and Malcolm X all wrapped up in the Jim Crow south.

New in the graduate program for English at the University of New England, I found graduate housing near the Biddeford campus in Portland, Maine. I shared a two-bedroom apartment with three other students, Ben Cannon from New York City, Laura Warren from Boston and Lindsey Jordan from California. My $110 stipend covered my $90 portion of the rent. Ben had his own room; Laura and Lindsey shared the other room. We shared the chores, and a fridge. I used the small back alcove for my room. Purple curtains secured my privacy. I rather the small space so I did not have to keep answering dumb questions from white people like, "How often do you wash your hair?" What is that greasy stuff you are putting on your hair?" "Why does your skin look grey in the winter?" I stayed to myself and they did not bother me, except when we watched the news about the Freedom Riders, sit-ins, and boycotts. They were eager to talk "race" when it was comfortable for them. They didn't see their own white privilege or racist's attitudes. How could they when they were so interested in my black Mississippi ass? How could they be racists because I lived with them, right? I thought the Klan was bad but liberal white people are the Klan turned inside out. I couldn't figure them out at least in the south things are obvious, in our face. This covert shit freaked the hell out of me, veiled on pasty white smiles. Maybe I should have stayed and fought in my community but I had to leave.

On campus many students engaged in important social, political, and economic conversations about identity, civil rights, social justice and democracy. Kathy Novak was the head of Women's Student Alliance for Democracy (WSAD). Kathy was a passionate redhead from Rhode Island. She made everyone around her a believer. I liked her. She was dedicated to changing the world. I welcomed the opportunity to save the world since I wasn't able to save MY world or myself. I also joined the Black Freedom for Justice, and the Writers Collective.

Getting back to Marva, I guess I am still processing what happened 23 years ago, somewhat confused and disturbed even after all these years. Kathy invited me to a meeting that addressed local political matters. Once a month WSAD hosted local groups to meet on campus so students could participate in the decisions. I entered the meeting of the League of Women Voters, immediately scanned the room for black faces. It was my first time at a women's political meeting. I saw about thirty white women mixed in with a few Asian women. They wore colorful T-shirts, shorts or flowery skirts and hiking sandals. They sat on the floor or sofas all intensely staring at the speakers from the local community. They were debating the efficacy of electing Thomas Rheingold--(Independent) given his record on teacher evaluation reform and hiring only male interns in his office. The conversation was heated at times but rather esoteric; devoid of any true substance beyond the obvious, "we need more white women in spaces". The issues of social class, power of whiteness and other substantive matters of education reform were never even brought up. White women, especially upper middle class ones are entitled but constantly pulled out the victim card. I quietly sat occasionally listened to them bitch and moan, at times glazed over thinking about my new apartment, my kooky roommates, should I bike to the farmer's market or attend yoga class in the morning.

Random thoughts raced through my mind I kept searching the space for any sign of familiarity--that's when I noticed Marva noticing me. I was pleased to see a sister at the meeting who didn't seem so strange. Her inviting smile was warm and friendly. Something about her intrigued me. Maybe it was her short 'fro or her fuchsia colored scarf artistically draped around her long neck or her brown honey skin, I found myself lost in her recognizable beauty for just that moment. I was lonely and missed black people. Marva reminded me how much I needed home and other faces of color. The committee chairwoman stated, "Ladies, thank you for attending tonight's meeting. Please make sure to sign in so we can follow up on tonight's agenda. Meeting adjoined." "Hi, I am Marva Whitman, you would be?" "I am Frances." "Frances, do you have a last name?" I gave an awkward smile and responded, "Frances Freeman, like in freeway." Marva sensed my discomfort; she laughed putting both of us at ease.

After the meeting we went to get a drink. We talked for hours about everything and about nothing. I was feeling high after my third drink. Before I knew it we were kissing right in the bar. Her tongue was softer than any man I had kissed before; the coconut shea butter from her hair was sweet. I was confused, groggy. After a few minutes I caught myself. I pulled away. I am not sure if I stopped kissing Marva because we were in public, or because we had just met or because I did not like it or because I liked how I felt. After that night we never really spoke much. She called me several times but I never called her back. I would make excuses whenever I saw her on campus. She said I was a tease, maybe I was, I just didn't know what I wanted at that time. Marva told me, "I don't have any desire to be your lesbian experiment, either you want this or not." For her things were cut and dry. I was unsure about love, sex, and myself. A part of my soul was gone but Marva did not know. For that I am sorry. Her scent lingers in my memory of another unfinished "project."

Back home now my head was filled with regrets, unresolved pain---jumbled. My aloneness was palpable.

Truth is every year when the wildflowers bloom I pause and remember that day. It's not as if I want to remember but it's important never to forget some things. It shapes and haunts me everyday. Maybe today I will bury the hurt, regret, pain and bitterness. Today is my funeral and I hope my resurrection.

My name is Frances Sue Freeman; my friends call me Franny, from Philadelphia, Mississippi. I still occasionally speak with an accent. My colleagues at the University of Vermont often correct my grammar or tell me I sound country. Assimilation from the south was a prickly process. It's been at least twenty-five years since I was home. After that day I never returned. There was nothing there for me after the incident. I regularly sent Mama money in a white envelope, no note just the cash, my signature on a blank sheet of paper and no return address. No matter how much I hated what she did she was still my mother.

I finished Campbell Teacher's College, in Jackson and worked with an elementary school as a substitute teacher. I was getting ready to move out of my Mama's home and find a permanent job teaching school. No colored young woman from my neighborhood ever left home unless she was a whore, a performer, a missionary, or was getting married. I didn't lead protests or speak out but in my soul I was a rebel behind my proper church girl appearance. I wanted Black people, especially children to live like all them fancy white people I would see driving round town. We were in the midst of the Civil Rights movement; integration and education were on the frontline. Brown vs. the Board of Education legally ended segregation in schools but poor black children were far from equal at that time. I knew I was smart and had enough will power to move a mountain I just needed to be in another place to do what was necessary; a place far from the Klan, racism of white people and the limited imagination of my own black community. Perhaps I should have stayed but I died on that day.

I was almost five months pregnant and just beginning to show. I began to hold my stomach in everywhere I went, especially around Mama and at church. I stopped singing in the young people's choir because the Sunday guilt was too much to bear. Mind you on Friday and Saturday I was having big fun—sinning my way into hell. No one knew I had this secret life, except the other girls in the choir because we were all living the lie. Christian hypocrites we fit right in at St. Paul's. I am still ambivalent about church and religion to this day. With role models like my Mama (aka Mother Freeman) sister so and so and brother what's his name I just can't stomach the idea of going to church. Mind you, I still believe in God, I'm just still hurt from what happened back in Mississippi. Worship was impossible because the hurt was too deep. Miss Ernestine Watkins, the only church woman

I trusted, would say, "Jesus don't want you when you up but when you down. Call on him chil' He'll answer you by and by." Miss Ernestine would go on to say, "Remember God don't make no mistake, He's good all da time." She certainly walked the walked. I hope I can find my way back.

I would do all my chores, prepare for class, and then go help Mama out at Mrs. Dodd's house. The Dodd's were typical Southern upper middle class white family. Mama was their maid. She cooked, cleaned and raised their four children. Many of my clothes were hand me downs from Mrs. Dodd. Mrs. Dodd would say, "Franny, I think it's nice to see you colored girls goin' to school." She didn't really mean it but she thought I would be impressed with her remarks. She had no idea how much I hated her. I kept smiling. White people like her only wanted to see you smile. I know she thought I should be a maid like my Mama. I was too glad to finish school and have options.

Mrs. Dodd and all her fancy society friends could go straight to hell. Surviving the south at that time meant saying "yes ma'am" and smiling like a good nigger.

Weekends were for my escape. For almost one year I would meet Albert Gilpen every Friday evening at exactly 6:30 p.m. by the bus stop. He never failed to meet me. He would say, "I don't believe in keeping sugar waiting 'cause she may melt all over the sidewalk." I met him one day when I was waiting for the bus to go home. I was a virgin, ready for the picking. Albert smelt my inexperience and took advantage of it---but I enjoyed it. He was a smooth talker. He had the brightest smile and pretty teeth. He was jet-black like rich oil. His hair was thick like course wool and his hands were like magic. We would go to Mr. Turner's old barn. I don't think I will ever forget how delightful Albert made me feel as we lay in the old barn making love over and over again.

It should have bothered me that he never took me out to eat. Albert always wanted to keep our "special secret" for us. I was certainly of age, 21 to be exact, finished school, had a job prospect and a plan to be somebody but I dare not disrespect my mama's home. He was my first lover, the secrecy made the sex even better. I wanted to savor each kiss, each caress, each drop of sweat and each promise of forever after.

I heard the talk in town that Albert had another woman. I did not want to believe that my Albert could even look at another woman. Because when he looked into my eyes he loved me. When I told Albert I was pregnant, things changed. He started to miss our regular rendezvous time. His touch became rough. Sweet kisses were now incredulous; his words tore at my flesh as a vulture devouring his prey. His eyes boiled with indignation. I did not plan the baby but I was not sad either. Denying this baby would amount to denying our love.

It was a Wednesday afternoon when I was helping Mama at Mrs. Dodd's home in a white suburb outside our Philadelphia community. I was feeling tired, my back ached. I could feel the baby moving more and more. I went to the bathroom and closed the door behind me. I did not know the lock was broken. Mama walked in on me. I can still see the shock on her face as she stared at my bulging stomach, full breasts and burgeoning life inside my unmarried womb. She couldn't speak for that moment, which at the time seemed like hours, because the rage she felt stifled her voice. She quickly slammed the bathroom door and ran to the kitchen. The force of the slam caused the bathroom mirror to shatter. I didn't know if I should follow her or run away.

I ran after her 'cause I wanted her to understand. When I got to the kitchen she was in tears. I said, "Mama please talk to me, please Mama." "I have nothin to sey to you whore. You no chil of mine! How culd you do dis to me? After I workin' at this white bitch's house to send you to teachin' college this is what you go and do! How culd you do dis." She then reached for a knife and came after me. I was paralyzed with fear, my heart raced. My mother was coming after me with a butcher's knife! She slashed and stabbed my stomach. I blocked her with my right arm but she kept coming after me. Blood covered Mrs. Dodd's clean floors. It was at that moment that I awoke from my daze and began running best I could, holding my stomach.

I ran out the door, Mama chased me with the knife in this white neighborhood, screaming, "You are a mother fucking whore!" I knew her voice but not know this woman. White people were going crazy. One o'clock in the afternoon two Black women screaming, cursing, waving knives, blood, and pregnant—a truly wild scene. The only place I thought I would be safe was with Albert. His house was seven long blocks away. Blood dripped down my thighs, legs and arm. I wasn't in pain because I was in shock. I was weak barely able to get to the front door. When I arrived at his house, a young woman answered the door. She was holding a baby and trying to calm down a toddler. She looked as though she knew who I was. I staggered, with a faint voice I said, "Excuse me, I'm Frances is your brother Albert home?" "My brother! Bitch, do I look like a god damn sister? I'm Albert's wife. You just like all the others that ring my door." I wanted to vomit but instead I asked her for help. I wanted to save my baby. "Please, can't you see I need help?" She responded, "I don't care if you and your bastard child die. Leave me and my man the hell alone."

By this time Mama had already arrived home. Mrs. Dodd fired her after the incident. Mama went on and on about what a disappointment I was to everyone at home. Daddy and Granddaddy were the only ones who cared. Granddaddy got in his truck and went looking for me. I had gone into labor and started vomiting along a dirt road.

My mother and my man were both dead to me at that point. I was alone, except for my dear Granddaddy and my father. And I was going to lose my baby. Granddaddy found me lying in a patch of purple wildflowers. He took me to the local colored hospital. It was too late for the baby. My Granddaddy told me that I died for a minute. I stayed with my older brother Hodges and his family while I recovered. To this day I have never stepped foot back in my Mama's house.

My brother Hodges was an alcoholic; he's dead now. His wife, Mattie Lee, is a midwife. I don't know how they got together. She is soft-spoken quiet—almost invisible. She liked to be needed. She's one of those sick nurturing women who only feel valid if they are saving people. I always swore to myself that I was never going to be that kind of woman. Mind you I was pleased to have her take care of me but who wants all that impecuniousness.

Mattie Lee and Hodges had two children, Buster and Lena. Hodges and I barley spoke growing up but there was a silent code of family if either one of us needed anything the other tried to help. While Hodges' only friend was the bottle generally his heart was good. Mama always thought he was a good for nothing nigger. I think it's because he reminded her of our daddy. I'll get to daddy later. Hodges left home when he was 14. Considering all that a young black man had to go through, especially in the south in the 1950s, he did all right.

Buster, my nephew, at that time of this incident was six years old. He was a fair skinned delicate little boy. Other children often teased him for his girlish ways. He was always so sensitive to animals, and any kind of suffering. While I recovered he would brush my hair and rub my face. Buster's gently ways endeared me to him. He's now living in New York where he is a musician. I think when he came out of the closet (inspired by James

Baldwin) is what killed his daddy. Hodges blames himself for not being a good role model for his son. But Buster, no Buddy (that's his new name) was going to be gay no matter what and Buddy is the best part of Hodges.

I remember Lena's indifference towards me. Even at eight years old she conveyed her disapproval of her father and me through her distance. She is still in Mississippi, devoted to her mother and the church. She is a nurse and plans to be married next year. I wish Lena and I were as close as Buddy and I, but I've learned not to expect much in life from people. Lena gave me what she wanted and I accepted her love on her terms. Worthlessness was part of my penance.

I am a woman with few family connections to other women. Part of me learned to hate myself for being black and female. I have struggled with loving myself. Not having my Daddy around didn't help. My Mama and Daddy were never married. His name was Frank people called him Frankie. I was named after him. He had eight children, including Hodges and myself, and three women. I only knew three of his other children—Heather, Claudine and Marvin. These were Dorothy's children. Dorothy was a nice lady. She was so beautiful, like Lena Horne, glamorous. All of Daddy's women lived within a one-mile radius in Mississippi.

When my Daddy heard that Albert didn't want anything to do with me he paid Albert a visit that same night I lost my baby. Daddy, drunk as a skunk went to Albert's house at 11:30 p.m. that Wednesday night. He had a bottle in one hand and a shotgun in another. The police report said, "Frank Freeman entered the premises at 1127 Cunningham Drive, resident of Albert and Betty Gilpen, approximately 11:30 p.m. on Wednesday, November 22, 1957. The assailant Frank Freeman shot four bullets, fatally wounding Mr. Gilpen. No one else was injured. Suspect was arrested. He did not resist arrest."

Even though Daddy didn't give me much growing up, that night he gave me more love than anyone else ever did. He gave me his life. Albert and his unborn baby died November 22, 1957. One killed by my mother the other by my father. They sentence Daddy to life in prison. After only five months in prison he killed himself. He would tell me, "Frankie lived as a man and is going to die like a man." We became close those last few months of his life. After I recovered I would visit him in prison. He would tell me about prison, "Frances, it's sick in here, men with men. It ain't natural to be locked up this way. I want to die like a man." I asked him if he loved Mama. Daddy said, "Loving a woman is a funny thing. You can't never love no woman." 'Cause once you do dey got you. I loved your mama's strength, her fight. She didn't take no shit from no one, including me. I loved her fight. You remind me of her." I sure didn't want Daddy to tell me that. I thought Mama and I were so different.

Officials at the prison said, "Mr. Frank Freeman died on Saturday, April 25th, 1958 at 6:45 p.m. The cause of death was ruled as a suicide." Never really knew what happened just knew that my Daddy was dead. He was finally free. All of this because I was pregnant, I sinned. I don't think I could ever forgive myself or mama for killing Daddy.

When I told Mama that Daddy was dead she tried to pretend that it didn't bother her none but I saw a tear in her eye. I knew she loved him because years before I overheard her talking with her girlfriends about him, "Girl, Frankie culd make me sing. He would always hit my spot." They would laugh. Maybe she just liked screwing him. But that can be enough when it's all you got.

After I gave my mother the news of Daddy's death I left Mississippi and never returned until today. Today is my Mama's funeral. I had to come even though we had not spoken a word to one another in over two decades something in my spirit pulled me back to this place. I have to make peace, peace with my Mama, Albert, my baby, and my demons. I have to get it right because life in Vermont is killing me. Marva was only the beginning of the many unfinished relationships; projects left on my shelf of ravaged opportunities.

Purple wildflowers were in full bloom. The old church is gone, burned down during KKK wilding raids in the late sixties. Three congregations now share this new church. Wildflowers lined the walkway to the church, I gathered a handful and placed them in my purse. I walked up to the open casket to view my mother's remains. Mama lost so much weight. Her round face was sunken in her ash casket. Her thin grey hair was tightly curled. She wore a pale yellow suit with her white gloves, pearl earring and matching necklace. I stood there numb, a stranger and her daughter.

I had to believe that Mama was so hurt that she stabbed me. Her own untold story of abuse is what she turned on me. Her life was a lie until the day she stabbed me. She wanted to leave the bondage of servitude; she feared I would end up alone in a hot Mississippi casket at the end of my journey. In her way she was setting me free with her faded truth, she was now unburdened. I would have had to care for a child whose father denied him and live my life as the other woman; in many ways the way my own mother lived. I don't think I would have left Mississippi if it weren't for that day. Maybe if I stayed I would have become the best elementary school teacher in town, married a preacher and had two babies. I don't know, regrets are poisonous to the soul. I have dined on bitter arsenic regrets throughout the years. I tried to create a new life as a professor, writer and one of only three tenured Black faculty in my university. I have traveled to eight countries and have friends all over the world but I am not whole.

The organist entered, he began to softly play "He's Sweet I Know, He's Sweet I know." I swore I heard my daddy's voice. "Franny time to fly, you is free." My niece and nephew came in and gave me a respectful hug. Buddy beckoned for me to sit with the family but I stayed in the back of the church. I waited for the crowd to come but there were only 25 people in the church. I just kept staring at Mama; unexpectedly tears began to fall down my cheek. Everything poured out of me. My child, daddy, Albert and Mama were in that ash coffin. I cried for over an hour. At the graveside as they lowered the casket the sun was bright ushering in a promise of newness. I took the crumpled wildflowers out and gently let them fall on my Mama. She was laid to rest with the truth that I had forgiven her covered with purple wildflowers.

"Papa used to shake his head at this and sey, 'What's de use of me taking my fist to a poor weakly thing like a woman? Anyhow, you got to submit yourself to 'em, so there ain't no use in beating on 'em and then have to go back and beg 'em pardon.'"

Zora Neale Hurston, except from Dusk Tracks on a Road in <u>I Love Myself When I Am Laughing</u>, p. 34.

Nikki Devon----Pale Blue Shades

For almost four years I have lived my life behind my pale
blue shades. Cool. Distant. Alone. I keep my shades on
whenever I am outside, day or night, even at home when
I have company over. It is my trademark, my thing.

My hair is usually wrapped or twisted, natural easy and
free. Rings on all my fingers, and one on my toe.
Midnight blue eyeliner frames my almond shaped eyes.
Eyes that are hidden behind my pale blue shades.
Headphones always on my ears. Jill Scott's lyrics soothe
my soul as I walk along the road. Walking behind my
pale blue shades. Distant. Cool. Alone. Nineteen years
old.

My mother is a lawyer. She just became partner at the
firm. She is bad. She works crazy hours. But we have
email, cell phones, and lots of technology to keep the
love flowing. So I walk down the street behind my pale
blue shades, listening to Jill Scott, and talking to my
mom's on my cell. Cool. Distant. Alone.

I work at a telemarketing company 25 hours a week.
Talking to strangers about this and that. I sit in front of
the computer, with my pale blue shades, listening to Jill
Scott, and talking to my moms. Cool. Distant. Alone.

Four years ago, before I started wearing my shades, I was
15 years old. It was the last time my daddy touched me.
For 10 years, two to four times a week my father would
molest me. Touch me, lick me and fuck me. My mama
knew but she did nothing. For ten long years he raped his
only daughter. I said nothing. I did nothing. Until one day
he was fucking me and he had a heart attack and died.
Right on top of me. His 250-pound fat body just dropped

on top of me. I rolled him off of me and I laughed. I just laughed. That's when I knew God had to be a woman.

We buried him five days later.

Before the services I went shopping for something to cover my shame, my guilt, my hate and my rage. I found these pale blue shades at Macys. I have kept them on since that day. Cool. Distant. Alone. Behind my pale blue shades.

"Being a woman is hard work. Not without joy and even ecstasy, but still relentless, unending work. ... The woman who survives intact and happy must be at once tender and tough. She must have convinced herself, or be in the unending process of convincing herself, that she, her values, and her choices are important."

Maya Angelou, Wouldn't Take Nothing For My Journey Now (p.6)

Mother Africa
By Sidney Wilfredo King III

Identity Crisis

Who me? Love you?
How can I love you when I lost myself in the shades of
my blackness?
How can I love you when I lost myself in the
Size of my hips?

Shades of blackness
       Light/medium/dark/midnight black
       Yellow/cinnamon/mocha/almond/coffee

I have come inside myself and out again
To find six degrees of blackness.

House sisters and brothers—light/redbone
But what about Uncle Clarence
Movement brothers and sister—dark panthers
But what about Sister Catherine

Small lips
Full lips
Thick lips

Hair   goodandbad   hair
Long and short   goodandbad   hair
Weave   luster silk   jheri curls
       braids
Natural and processed   goodandbad
       Goodandbad   goodandbad   hair

Who me? Love you?
How can I love you when I lost
Myself in them and my own self-hate
Identify yourself
Identify yourself   Identify
Who am I? Who are you?
Yes I am the off spring of the master's rage.

Yes I am the product of glamour and Ebony magazines
But
I am also the daughter and son of the
Red clay of the soil that gave birth to this planet
The sweet smile of the Afrikan sun
Has kissed my face
I am the daughter and son of Queen Mekeda and King
Halle Salasse
I am the dark one of the rich cocoa mountains
My soul springs up from Lake Victoria and my ancestors
sing for the Valley Nile
My wide hips bore the children of this planet
My breasts nourished the soil of all the children
My full juicy lips kissed the pain of whips and chains
away with a love supreme

Put down the wall
      Love ourselves   love   love
Put down the walls
      Identify yourself   and stop the
      Crisis
          Stop the crisis
              Stop the crisis   Stop

"Though you cannot climb the mountain steep and high;
You can stand within the valley as the multitude goes by
You can shout as happy melody as they slowly pass along
Though you may forget the singers but you'll never forget
the song."
80, Vera W., daughter of a schoolteacher, Arkansas

"I put away some food for us for later.... after the
preacher leaves."
Angela L., Cowpen, South Carolina

Cleaning Woman's Left Foot
(Dedicated to all the women who wash floors)

Tapping on the hard wood floor/tap/tap/tap
Slap ball change/slap ball change/dancing on the hard
wood
Tapping on the hard wood floor
Tingling   throbbing   throughout
My thigh
          Tapping on the hard wood floor
Unwanted kisses/grabbing and throwing
Tapping on the hard bedpost
Hips wide cushion his blows
Tapping/tapping on the hard bedpost

Wanting warm water to soak my feet from
Tapping on the white man's hard wood floor
Aching from standing, scrubbing
Cleaning and tugging
Tapping/tapping
Tapping on someone else's hardwood floor.

"Judge a person by their actions not their words."
Arnethia D., Bluefield, Virginia

Sticks and Stones

I
Nigger/bitch/whore/Mammy/Jezebel
Sapphire/kutch/cunt/trick/shorty/baby/dame/lady
O-man/gal/girl/pussy/pickney/kutchy/hutchy
Chick/jigga boo/darky/nappy/ugly

II
Criminal/drug pusher/stupid/shifty
Loud/silly/lazy/crooked/thief/dumb
Idiot/crazy/crack head/pimp/hustler
Shady/

III
What's in a name?
My name is Queen Mother Moor
Lovely creator of pyramids and temples.
Inventor of mathematics, astrology, medicine,
engineering and architect
Spiritual warrior
Healer
Priest
Chief
Teacher
Hannibal/Malcom/Sojourner
My name is mother/father
Grandmother/grandfather
Auntie/uncle
Sister/brother
Daughter/son
President
Manager
Artist
Nurse
Singer

Freedom fighter
Liberator

IV
My name is life
Call me by MY name

Shades of Me
by Stephen B. Ellis

BODY, LOVE, SEX & MEN

To My Afrikkkan Brothers

I
Know My spirit
　　　　　Woman/feminine/masculine/soft/strong
　　　　　Strong/soft/masculine/feminine/woman

You and I are one but two
Equal but different
　　　Know My spirit

II
Deep inside my womanness you/me/we
　　　Come
The Center of me brings forth life
Jealous you stand w a i t i n g your turn
To oppress me

Womb/womb ancestors before
　　　Still present
　　　　　　And eternal after
All come from my center my womanness

Powerless you stand w a i t i n g to spill
Your seed with the next and the next and the next

My brothers your seed is useless without my womb
But I am just a shell without you

So how are we men and women if we bring forth no
life???

III
Fathers with daughters
Brothers with sisters
Uncles with nieces
Teachers with students
Lovers with friends

71

Preachers with members
    Yet/but
        WE   We
                        We   we
      we
    Continue to love you
Hating you but twisted with guilt
    You raped us
    Took at will
    Abused our spirits

IV
Hate/anger
    Fear/shame
        The midnight wolf hollows at the
        Moon
        Grieving our lost innocence
Protector, we wait for you
    My Afrikkkkkkkkkan brother, where are you?
"Look inside my sister the Proctor is within/above/all
around."

V
Repair our pain, hide the shame
    Stand tall true sister
    Stand tall

VI
Know MY spirit

    Neck twisting/eye rolling/hip swaying
    Finger snapping/hand waving
    AT-TI-TUDE
    Strong/soft/masculine/feminine/woman
Evolving to the same as yesterday
        Resilient
Evolving womanness
    Ask me my brothers

Don't assume to know MY spirit
"Killing me softly with his song."

VII
Brothers respond
        "Bitch/mother fucker/cock sucking whore/
        Suck my dick"
        "Just another bitch with an attitude"

VIII
Wonder no more
        Killing me softly….softly
        Killing me dead.

IX
Can't stop loving you my brothers
        We know you/hate you
Can't stop loving you.
Nikki told you how we loved you
Alice once said you were a "Black Prince."

Can't stop loving you
But we still remember yesterdays
        And what about those white girls?

We remember you from our womb
        The center of our womanness and all
        Humanity

We remember how you lost your dignity
        No longer a man but chattel
        $3/5^{th}$s human
We remember your pain
        We watched you beaten
            And what about those white girls?

We remember how you touched us
        And we said NO
We remember you 'yo baby.
        Can't stop loving you

And what about those white girls?

X
Always in the background
    Baking your sweet potato pies

    Meeting is called to order
"Sing a song dear sister then sit your big ass down."

    Truth be told we listened to that
    Boring, long, same old speech of yours
    2, 3, 10 times and again
Always in the background

    BUT WE WILL BE HEARD

XI
The circle is closing back to our center
    "How do you love a Black Woman?"
You and I are one
    Different but equal, equal, EQUAL
Hold us tight in your strong arms
    Listen to us cry
    Know that we love you my Afrikkkkkkkkkkkan
brother
Be patient with us
    We too have fallen into the oppressor's trap.

XII
Know My spirit
    Woman/feminine/masculine/soft/strong

    Can't stop loving ME

    "Don't share your belly with people."
    90, Gladys Wint, Jamaica, West Indies

74

Baby Sue's Sonnet

Man, What Do I Want?
I want you to want me
Want me to love me
To kiss me.
I want you to want to taste my lips
My thighs, my toes
My (*pause... laugh*)
Want to kiss me all over and
Then do it all over again.
I want you to want to
Screw me, fuck me and make love to me
All in one night.
I want you to want to
Tell me your secrets, hopes and dreams.
I want you to want to
Hear my news about my day.
I want you to want me so much that
When you are driving down the turnpike you
Cum at merely remembering my scent.
I want you to want to linger in my embrace for at least
Three long minutes.
I want you to dance close to me and grind me like
Those good old days in the basement red light parties.
I want you to just hold my hand and not say a word.
I want you to look in my eyes and see my soul.
I want you to join me in a hot tub of bubbles
And sip cool wine and watch the candles melt as we
Are lost in some other place, and warm water is washing
over
Our weary bodies.
I want you to play your blues harmonica to me while we
lie
On a lily covered hill watching blue jays fly by.
I want you to walk in the rain with me.

I want you to love me when you are mad at the man or
Pissed at the bills.
I want you to be my friend and my lover.I want you to
want to hear my thoughts on Nietzsche, Dante, Hagel,
Achebe, Paul the Apostle, Audre Lorde and yes,
Sleepless in Seattle.
I want you to not trip out when I do my hair
Roll it, twist it, wrap it, press it, perm it and even cut it
I want you to still love me weaved, wigged or
Bald headed.
I want you to want me this much because,
Man,
This is how much I want you.

Rebe's Regrets

He was so beautiful
So fine.   So fine.
A smart man. Not the kind just filled with useless words
from dead people
But he could make poetry and philosophy out of the
music of Dizzy, Miles and Coltrane.
He was so beautiful.
A bad brother.
We would lay on his bed and vibe to the music.
After that we would make love on the futon
It was a smooth groove. Our naked bodies
Spooned around one another, close and tight
He was a good brother.
He could hold me for hours
He was a good brother   so beautiful.
On my 25th birthday made me dinner. Served
Me curry chicken, roasted potatoes and mixed greens in a
black tuxedo then
Took me dancing,
Gave me a diamond ring in a glass
Of champagne. "Marry me baby," he said.
I cried. I knew I could not marry him.
He was so beautiful. A bad brother.
He was not ready for this baby
His life had a plan, a rhythm. No room for this baby.
This man, my man, was not ready to be a daddy.
He was unemployed, 22 years old and nervous about
finishing college.
The next Tuesday afternoon my girl, Debra, took me to
the clinic
He was not ready for this baby
He was so beautiful
Ten weeks my child grew inside of body
My baby knew my voice

She knew my soul
But I could not do it to my beleaguered unemployed
Black man
I could not tell my man
He was a bad brother. He had a future.
I wasn't going to be another sister with an
Angry baby daddy resenting me.
I knew he was a good man.
I had to make this choice
No baby/ no drama/ no pressure
Or so I thought
Afterwards…
We listened to the music as I relax on his bed
Uncomfortable silence entered the
Peaceful space of tranquility
I could not talk to him as I did before.
His eyes knew there was an emptiness
In my heart.
I had to say adieu.
A good brother tossed away.
I loved him so.
I miss my baby
I miss my man.

*"Never have a single woman tell you how to keep your
man."*
Anonymous

Pretty in Pink

Pink ribbons tied
To black twisted wombs
Tumors throbbing
Black nipples and breasts
Lump found left breast
BARC 1 test positive
Trial drug guinea pig
Insurance pre-certification denied
Bills mounting daily
Experiment on me
No money to fight
Cancer for real
Radiation today
Chemo on Saturday
Fasting on Wednesday
Surgery on Thursday
"Ma'am, you really don't need your breasts anymore"
81 years old-diagnosis positive
Lymph nodes must go
Breast tissue gone

Now he hears his fate
PSA test
T cells rising
Too high
Just read Randy Pausch's
Last Lecture
Divine warning
Biopsy
Ultrasound
CAT-scan
Potions and prodding
"Are you next of kin?"
"We did the best we could."

Life won't be the same
Catheters
IVs
Surgery on Monday
Back to Bible Study on Thursday

Cancer birthday party
Son flown in from
Iraq
Cancer you are my blessing
My son is now home
But now you must go
Fight for your country

Leukemia, Lymphoma
Bone marrow
Transplant
Iron replacement

I knew I was sick

While I fight for
My life
Pink ribbons
And bows
Tied like nooses
To our necks
Susan G. Komen
Run from
Planned parenthood
Prohibit funding
Pick and choose
Who you cure
Race for a cure
Keep running
Pretty in pink

Pink roll call
Too many to call
We fight on
We run on
We love on
Bald
Bold
Beautiful
Pretty in pink

Little Miss Perfect

"Little Miss Muffet
Sat on a tuffet,
Eating her curds and whey,
Along came a spider,
Who sat down beside her
And frightened Miss Muffet away"

"Sit up straight, Patience!
Little ladies cross
Their legs."
Gracefully glide
Across the floor
Coy smile
Accents your
Feminine allure
Rote silicone responses
Rattle out,
"Thank you"
"Please"
"Excuse me"
"Of course I can wait"
"No, it isn't any trouble."
Silently boiling in
Patriarchal pots
"Hold your tummy in."
My curls get in the way

Tired from smiling, tucking
Pulling, plucking
Spanxing, binding
Crossing, waxing
Shaving, dieting
Tired of tuffets and no
Muffins

Whey too much whey
Diet and then weigh
Perfect Patience
Envy of girls
Near and far
Behind the smile
Lace and gluten
Free whey

Seething still
In rage
Structures of oppression
Bylaws lead to bypass
By outs and good byes
Traditions like
Spider's webs
Won't frighten Patience
Away.

Eating misogyny away
Conformity, provocative
Images away
Binging and purging
Patience vomits it
Away.

Sitting on her settee
Eating whatever she dares
Scales of success
Measurements of
Progress dissolves
Little Miss Perfect away.

"Spring break is broken Friday the 13th 2009"
(Dedicated to all the women who do for others)

Today there is a heaviness
That weighs me down
The sun shines outside
But deep within there is a
Tired weariness
My soul screams for
Sunshine within

I have given so much
To others that my pool has run
Empty
Have I forgotten to pray?

Should I have fasted so I could
Feel the Son shine
His face within my soul?

"Fast and pray"
Grandmother's words
And "God will show up"

But here I am
Resenting spending my spring break
Working for the cause
To liberate
Others
I have forgotten to liberate myself
Forgotten to rinse out the
Cobwebs in my mind and finish a good book

Tied to clocks, deadlines, responsibilities
Can I, if I wanted to
Just

Enter this computer screen
Reboot my dreams
Restart my vision
Input a new screensaver

Pulling at me
Wanting to talk to
Someone out loud
Not online, no more emails
No more Facebook

Who has time to
Just sit and listen
Who helps the sister that gives
Catch air?

"Fast and pray"
Grandmother's words
And "God will show up"

Jump in this box
Circle only one answer
Check only one
Who are you?
Where do you fit?

I want to check
All the boxes
Check all of the above

An odd woman
Raised around men and boys
With strong mother, father
And grandmother
With accents

Different and alone
Not old enough
To stroll down Civil Rights memory lane
Not girly enough to go to the mall
Too old to understand Cold Play
Not man enough to attend your members' only meetings

Body daily growing older
Arthritis, pinched nerves
Falls from running too
Fast to please and be loved
Injuries from trying
To prove I belong
Pains from injuries
When I used to fly
Hair blowing in the breeze
Dancing and sliding
Striding just right
Those were the
Days

Jump in this box
Circle only one answer
Who are you?
Why are you so hard to
Fit?

Too well educated
Too loud
Too quick with the wit
Talk too much
Too many words
Too many cookies, chips and hips
Too needy
Just too, too, too much for anyone to hear

Not perfect enough
Pack them away
Bury them deep
Feelings of aloneness

Illusions of community
Dissolve When I feel all
Alone

Spring break
Is busted and over
What will I have to say?

Where have I gone?
What stories can I share?

Maybe it is in this moment
When I face
My truth that I need a real break
That
I will begin to feel the sun/Son shine
On my soul

"Fast and pray"
Grandmother's words
And "God will show up"

When spring break ends....
Clock ticks
Pick up the kids
Buy print cartridges
Prepare to speak
Put gas in the car

Check on folks
Worse off than me

Worse off than me…

Put a smile on my face
Move past
These feelings
Quickly

The clock is ticking
Spring break is over

Remix…
Tomorrow is here
God showed up just
In time

FRIENDSHIP & SISTERHOOD

Shanay Shafequka Tamia Watkins

I
Orange and purple acrylic two-inch nails decorated
With diamond rhinestones
Neck shaking
Head waving
Gum chewing
Her second glass of Absolute is
Poured as she waits for Ricki Lake to start
Burgundy silicone gel wrap surrounded by
Blonde cornrows
Faded green and red butterfly tattoo
Cover the black and blue tattoo of Quami's daddy's
name.
Butterfly flies over her right stretch marked sagging
breast
A size 12 black spaghetti strap top
Encase her almost size 20 brown body
Matching black spandex pants and gold sandals complete
the
Ensemble

II
Tequon, Quami, and Teneka holler for lunch.
Their Captain Crunch, chocolate yahoo, grape and cheery
fruit roll ups and orange aid breakfast has lost its
nutritional value.
Grabbing toys, writing on the walls, watching Jerry
Springer.
10, 8, and 6 year olds summer vacation escapades.
Granny promised us Checkers French fries and Popeye's
chicken today.

Granny's cigars aggravate their asthma but a little cough won't kill them.

III
Shafequka gets to Rite Aid by 2:00 p.m.
Pay day today. Need new tracks, nails need fixing,
The Limited has a sale. Teneka's medicine is in, Quami
Has to go to the dentist that's a $10 co-pay. Tequon needs
Some sneakers. Remember the freezer is empty.

IV
Kwali, her man, is taking her out to a new club
Round the way
He's 24, she's 22
They met at Rolland's Bar three weeks ago.
He always got money and his gold teeth make him look
so fine and rich.

Can't worry 'bout the kids
Granny has to watch them tonight.

V
Granny checking her watch
She's got a date tonight
34 years old still fits in her
High school prom dress. Granny got to get her groove on.
Her tracks need a touch up too.

VII
Tequon, Quami, and Teneka filled with
Greasy fries and chicken, and candy
Played three hours of game boy, six hours of talk shows,
Soap operas and cartoons
Went to hang out with some other kids.
Granny don't know them but it gave her a break from
The madness.

Cigar smells in their clothes and hair

VIII
No stories
No hugs
No laughter
No swings in the park
Where will they be tonight?
Granny's got to groove
Mama's got a man

IV
Tequan's daddy's dead
Quami's daddy's moved away
He visits when he can
Tenekas's daddy in the Army
He comes home on leave
Where will they be tonight?

Shanay Shafequka Tamia Watkins
Had three little kids she didn't know what to do.
Each got a daddy
Nowhere to be found
Shanay Shafequka Tamia Watkins
Loves her three babies
And doesn't know what to do?
Tequon, Quami, and Teneka snuggle with
Their Mama tonight.
Kwali will have to wait.
Shanay Shafequka Tamia Watkins wants
A little love. Can you help her out some nights?

By Paul el Sadate

Market Women—All is Well

I

Clothes on her head. She walks a mile to fetch water to wash clothes and boil the dumplings and green bananas. She meets her friends at the well. Hear news of what's going on around the village. "Odassa, wha' say? Mi se ya luk fat 'n nice. Di man treat ya right?" " Mi si. Nice." Odassa likes this routine because she sees other women like herself with pitchers on their head. "Marcia, ya haf any ripe banana? Or bread fruit?" "Yes, but mi na giv yu nun. 'Member las time you tek mi fish u did promise fi give mi bak but you is nutin but an ole teaf!" Women all laugh because they know Cynthia's tricks. But she is still loved by the women at the well.

"Mi nu care. Yu nutin' but an ole heffa! Yu ugly bitch!" "Chrissy, why ya hafa 'cause trouble?" Odassa comments. "Mi?" Hush Chris, hush. Neva min dem gal. How is Winston?" "You si how nice and fat I get? Right. Marcia, ya here mi? Mi have a gud man." "Chrissy, u tek any man." Marcia scolds Chrissy for her promiscuity. "Watch hair, mi body is nice and mi know how fi get de man dem. So, Marcia, tak yu green banana an gu wey." All the women laugh. They continue to trade fruits and vegetables, humming and laughing.

II

"Carry mi ackee go a Linsted Market not a quaty worth cent
Carry mi ackee go a Linsted Market not a quaty worth cent"

Market Reprise
III
Sweet mango trees

East Indian, Bombay, turpentine, number 11, beef
mango
Black mango, hairy mango, ladyfinger, Saint
Julian
Plums ripe and ready
Rosemary by the riverside
June plum, coolie plum tree
Red coat and yellow coat plum
Apples anyone?
Ethiopian apple, star apple, rose apple,
Naseberry, stinky toe, custard apple, soar sop,
Sweet sap, paw paw and jack fruit

IV
Gal, get u fruit, nice and sweet.

Friends By and By

Crystal vases adorned with peach roses
neatly placed on mahogany mantles
cascading colored candles
warm bright bone china
laughing friends watch
hickory wood burning in
brass framed fireplaces
singing Stevie Wonder songs
telling tall tales of conquests
political progress
and
plans to save the race
baby boys join in the fun
babbling baby banter
bouncing along
eating tomato salad, couscous, pan seared tuna,
asparagus, goat cheese, crackers and sweet potato pie
Merlot lingers on our tongues
blessed friends, good friends,
sister friends, brother friends,
share sweet home
memories by and by.

Sister Mother-less, Mother

No baby you bore, better are we
We suck from your tits without
A moment
To notice
Mother-less mother you mother
Us
Us the takers
Us the breakers
Us the no good brother haters
Us the church going heathens
Us the critics
Us the judgers
Us the professional know it all sisters

Sister, we pause
We glance notice your wanting stares
Gently loving our babies
We sometimes neglect these
Same old babies
They get on our nerves
Time and time again
You remind us to love

Mother-less sister, we pause
To notice
After we have sucked you dry
Dumped our babies on you
Whenever it suit us
To get a break from the
Motherhood grind
Resented you for freedom we lost

Sister, we pause

To notice
Your grace, gentle and calm

Mothering us
Loving us
Mother-less sister
We love you still

Time Stands Still, My Friend
(Dedicated to all my friends who know my heart)

Time suspended
Years passed
But there you are
As you were before
My friend.

Children/work/family
Illness and death
Pushes the clock
Winters' frosty air
Your voice whispers in my ear
Fragrant buds erupt
From the earth
I knew you were near
Blistering heat made
Cooler from your laughter
Deciduous trees
Amber leaves signal
Hibernation and
A faster moving clock
Back to school
Back to the grind

Missing my sister friend
You know me
You love me
So why can't I find time
For
You?
Because I carry you
Everywhere I go
Time stands still
Forever my friend

"Everyone you think is your friend is not your friend."
Wanda, Alabama

Sister Friends in My Head

Jill Scott

Her thick luscious
Afro, lips and hips
Transcended neo wanna be soul
Sisters like me
To a new place,
Jill Scott
You came the right time
For us
You cross our mind
Even as the haters hate
We hear your call
Lyrically spitting poetic
Curves in black beauty
Taking your freedom
Living your life
'Cause it's golden

India Arie

Dark beauty descendent of
Mende, Kru and Fula people
Sierra Leone, Liberia, Guinea-Bissau &
Georgia roots
Earthy words
Deep tones layered
Cocoa butter love
Doing your hair just
Doing you
Your brown skin
Shining from your grace
Wearing your Queenly crown
Striped down to

Pure acoustic soul
Naked
Open
Authentic beauty
Young sisters
Feel free to stare
Warning while you stare
Her pure beauty
May burn your eyes

Michelle O.

First lady swag
South side of Chicago
Rocking floral frocks
Digging up patriots' soil
Planting granddaddies' gardens
To feed
Body, mind and soul
Princeton, Harvard degrees
And President in tow
Purple J. Crew cardigan tied
Around your waist
Running to Target
Sasha and Malia need school supplies
Isabel Toledo/ Jason Wu/ Thakoon
Maria Pinto and Narciso Rodriguez
Wait in line to wrap
Haute couture fashion on
Our statuesque FLOTUS' frame
Dawn routine push-ups &
Flex
Keeping it real
In the White House
We love how you love our

Daughters and sisters
Remembering Hadiya Pendleton
Celebrating Gabby and Serena
Toned arms paying homage
To sisters who worked in the fields
Sisters who build families, communities
Not afraid to be you
Powerful
Dancing close with your
Boo, At Last
We have you, loving out loud
At last,
We have you.

FAITH & CHURCH

Church Time

Gotta put on my best 'cause its
Time to go to the house of the Laud
"Boy you betta gets outta that bathroom before I slap you upside
Your head
'Cause its time to go to the house of the Laud."

"'Nigga you comin' a church? You sure need
To get right with God."
You sure 'aint no good. You never got no money
Can't keep no job. You is one sorry nigga'.
Anyway I don't got no time for no mess today
'Cause its church time

"Praise the Laud Sista Bertha, sure is nice to see you"
        Child that is sure one ugly hat big butt Bertha wearing
I can't believe that tramp Vertimae got the nerve to sit in my seat.
        She don't come to choir practice or Pastor's Aide auxiliary meeting
I gotta get over there and give her a piece of my mind
But I have no time for that now
'Cause it worship time

These are the most hypocritical deacons I have ever seen
Deacon Wallace smoking, cussing and drinking hard liquor
I just have Colt 45
But that sure 'aint none of my business

This is the most dead worship music
Need some pick me up, maybe a little beat?
Like the one I heard last night at that Club

Oh my God, who is that brother over there?
What a blessing. He's looking this way
Let me sit up straight. Praise the laud he 'aint got no ring
on
Oh there goes Miss Leda sitting next to my blessing.

"Boy, I should have left you at home
With your worthless daddy"
He 'aint never going to marry me no way
So I gots to watch out for myself.

Women's Day, Men's Day, Pastor's Anniversary
First Sunday, Usher's Program, Choir Anniversary
Wear white, wear pink, wear black and white
Don't forget your corsage
It's church time it's church time
Time to get right with God
Please Rev. not too long today, its football season, its
spring, its summertime, it's raining, snow may be falling,
please not too long today.
Church time   Church time

Every Sunday the same old thing
But I trys never to miss a Sunday
Don't want to lose my blessing

*"Remember this is not your life you can always do
better."*
China W., daughter of a sharecropper

103

Purple Felt Hats

Where are the real grandmothers today?
Plum and fat
Purple felt church hats, flowered pink dress and white
dress shoes
Sunday's best carefully hung and wrapped each week
Hands rough from washing clothes
Ringing out laundry
Mixing starch for Mommy's uniforms and Daddy's white
shirts
Where are the grandmothers that cooked big pots of
porridge,
Grits, fried dumplings, macaroni and cheese, roast beef
potatoes carrots and gravy. Enough for an army just in
case someone stopped by.
Grandmothers that tell you, "Don't go to that boy's house
because
We don't know his mother" or "Don't ride your bike
Further than I can see you!"
Where are the grandmothers that can hold two children
and a baby all at the same
Time in her wide loving lap. These grandmothers always
had a song on their lips like, "Jesus loves the little
children." And told a nursery rhythm that was just like a
griot's rap.
Where are the grandmothers whose homes were always
spotless?
Dozen of knick-knacks and figurines lined up on the shelf
dusted and polished. Chairs and lamps covered with
plastic to protect their original luster and value.
Where are the grandmothers who combed our hair after
mother and father left for work? Colorful ribbons and
clips at the end of each plait and every part greased just
so to prevent the flaking and dandruff.

Grandmothers who planted tomatoes, potatoes, cabbage, sting beans, and corn then picked them when ripe for supper and gave some to the neighbors. Saving the best for dinner with the Reverend on Sundays.

Grandmothers who swept the front porch and sidewalk every morning after reading the Bible and praying for all in our home and church. The lesson would end with a verse from the Psalms.

No television just hymns played from the radio or stereo. Grandmothers who read the daily newspaper from cover to cover. They couldn't tell you where Calcutta was on the map but they knew about the suffering of its people. They sounded like Black people in the neighborhood. So they prayed for them too.

Where are those grandmothers we knew and we loved. Grandmothers who spoke wisdom in love and gentleness. Quiet yet firm, direct and assured.

With skin was soft from plain old soap and water with a little Vaseline at night.

Every morning hot herb tea, every night hot milk to go to sleep.

Clothes were hand washed and hung on the line to dry. Grandmother smelled of sunshine and roses, mint and strawberries.

Where are those grandmothers who separated house clothes from going to the doctor clothes, church dresses from dinner with dresses with friends? Grandmothers who always had a drawer with her best panties, bras and nightgowns. Ready for a stay in the hospital overnight. Never afraid of death to come. The Lord was her safety net.

Grandmothers who listened to your stories over and over again even when you were grown she asked you the same thing before she hung up the phone, "What's for supper tonight?" Always happy to hear about your news of promotions, vacations and publications but cared more about your health and your spirit.

"Grandmother, why don't you get married again?" I would ask her time and time again. "Child I have had my fun, no regrets for me. Besides I don't want to have to iron, sew, cook, for no man again." Where are the grandmothers at peace with themselves, forgiving, loving well adjusted and elegant, with purple felt hats.

"Good morning to you. Good morning to you. We all in our places with sun shining faces. This is the way to start our new day. Good morning little boyzies. It is time to get up."
Attorney, Junius Williams, Richmond Virginia

Adhan, A Call to Prayer

Leaving Golden Crust with my warm afternoon chicken
patties in a small white bag and sliced hard dough bread
the crisp spring cold barely caused a chill. My yellow
wool scarf covered my cheeks. The bright sunshine
remained me that it was spring.

Walking back to my dirty black Ford escape, the call to
prayer rings out from the yellow and green mosque on the
corner. The Imam offers the adhan. His voice sings the
haunting, ancient call to prayer.

I fight my instinct to kneel on the sidewalk and lower my
head in prayer. Why was the sound today so compelling
to my Christian soul?
Flashbacks to afternoon walks along bustling Cairo
streets seared in my memory.

The savory smell of curry chicken wrapped in golden
crust quickly jolts me back to the Newark neighborhood.
The Imam's voice now gone
Returning to my car the ride is done with me in a daze,
Everything the same but for a moment the blue and white
I-hop sign on the left eerily pulls my eyes to stare and
think of the blood splattered floor roped off with
yellow caution tape.

A call to prayer, pray for mothers burying sons, for
grandfathers burying daughters, pray.
A call to prayer, ancient chant, calling us to rise and
stand.
Rise to stand, to bend and to pray.
Bended mothers never broken
Bending to pray.

"Father, I stretch forth my hands, no other help I know."

Sunday Morning Rain

Pat, pat, ting
Pat, ting, ting
Raindrops on the zinc
Roof
Rooster crows.
Ping, ping
Cock a doodle, do
Raindrops
Morning cool fresh.
Sea clean scent
Ting, ting
Ping
Chocolate tea, nutmeg
Cinnamon
Fresh
Cock a doddle, do
Sun rises
Ping
Rain
Drops
Stop
Breadfruit roasting
Ackee and salt fish
Ribbons in hair
White straw hat
Carnelian slip below my
Yellow dress
Sunday breakfast
Time to worship
Ting, Ting, Ting
Raindrops stop

The Source of Our Strength

Thou are my blessing, my very help in times of troubles
Your Righteous will never be forsaken
Marvelous through times of change
Marvelous in my eyes
Fragile hearts can praise her
Come as you are
Dress code not required just an open heart
Hallelujah
Thank you Jesus
You are my help, my deliverer.
My light in darkness
In times like these we need an anchor
A savoir to take us over trouble waters
Grace and mercy rescue us from our fate
Teach us Lord to wait on you and trust on you
Even when our heart is heavy and the storms are
Raging around give us power to move mountains.

You safely carried my ancestors from the Motherland
To an evil strange land. You kept us near glory
We will trust you even now as AIDS, guns,
Prostate cancer, heart disease, diabetes, sickle cell,
colonialism,
Imperialism, capital punishment, drugs, racism, sexism,
heterosexism,
Broken families, hunger, and self hate run ramped in our
Communities.

No weapon formed against me or my people shall ever
prosper.
I will survive
I will survive
We   will   survive
We   will   survive

I will	praise		Him	
I will	praise		Him	
We		will		praise Him
We		will		praise Him

The devil is already defeated
The devil is already defeated
I already have the victory
My sons have already won the victory
My great grandchildren are already victorious

The God that I serve is awesome,
Loving, mighty, all powerful, She/He/they are everything
to me.

JUSTICE

Lilies in the Fields (dedicated to my students in Black Womanhood 4/25/01)

You walk in the room. All I can see is a bitch and whore. Why can't I see Fannie or Bette, Gwendolyn Brooks or Ida, Harriet, Sojourner, Zora or Barbara Jordan? Blinded by capitalism, imperialism, sales at Saks Fifth Ave., Jet's beauty of the week and Janet's new waistline. Why when you walk in the room can't I smile just to think that could be Nikki, Sanchez, Yuri or Coretta. Your tits are bigger, hair is longer, and your man must be richer than mine.
Integrationist insisted that life would be sweeter it only has gotten milkier. Sister, why can't I see reunions and family, dumplings and lemonade, collard greens and turnips, Sunday morning praise and worship?
Why my sister when you walk in a room does my soul grow cold? Competitor not collaborator/ afraid you won't like my braids or my shoes.
You think you're so cute.
Why can't I feel your hurt and shame? Pain from his rage when his fist hits your face.
You enter the room and we watch and wait.
Lilies in a field of shit.

Society
By Sidney Wilfredo King III

112

Saturday Night Round Up

Tonight I heard sirens
Police, ambulances and fire engines in between the
Pop
Pop/ popping firecrackers and dog barks.
Sirens getting louder, more than just one
Ringing in my ear

Saturday night racing rescue to another building to save
another brown person.

My doors are shut, locked from within
My sons are accounted for
The death angel passes by

But someone's child, someone's mama
Someone's home is unsettled tonight
Suddenly changed without any notice

No more sirens for a minute or two
Someone else met a fate I hope not too bad
Tonight it was not me
Tomorrow I am not so sure

For now I count my blessings
1, 2
3, 4,…

Guilty Found Innocent/Innocent Guilty
(Written 1 week before the verdict)

Exoneration
Zimmerman may walk
'Cause Rachel don't know how to talk
Trayvon, stand your ground
Creepy ass cracker
Following behind
Paula Deen & Buddha pundits
Predict victory for
George
Stand your ground
For
Emmitt and Sean
Yosif, and Amadou
Stand your ground
Brown brothers
In skittles raids
Not in my backyard
Children captured
Justice denied
But still stand your ground.

Innocent young men
Yusef Salaam, Anton McCray, Kevin Richardson,
Ray Santana, Kharey Wise
Charged, convicted
Wilding Prosecutors
Creepy ass crackers
"Jurors what say you in the case of
George Zimmerman?"
"We have found him not guilty."

Trayvon you were found guilty
Rachel you were found guilty

Black brothers not on trial
You were found guilty
We know you were innocent
The glove does not fit
So acquit the brothers
Stand your ground.

The D is Silent

Django comic book metaphor
For a slave's resistance
Conceived in Quentin Tarantino's mind
Will not bring the truth to
Those locked up in
San Quentin Prison
Enslaved and chained up
Sam *Steeping Fetch* Jackson
Fighting Snakes on Planes
All pulp fiction
Like the textbooks
In failing schools

History lost
History contrived
Historical lies
By revisionists masters
On their race to the
Top

The d is silent in the
Master plan
D-eath by benign neglect
D-eliverance unattainable in viscous
Sludge of low expectations
D-eciding never to know the truth
D-aunted by d-eveloping brilliance

The d is silent in
Lion Gates/Weinstein Company/
Silent in Fox/MGM/Miramax Films

The d is silent in
Merchant Ivory/Sony/Kino International Corp

Paramount Pictures/Pixar/Walt Disney Pictures
Silent in Warner Brother Movies
Jamie apologetically boasting T-shirt of Trayvon
Martin's face
But chained to the
Pocket of mega
Masters
A Silent egomaniacal puppet
Dumb &
Deaf to the
Sounds of true
Liberation
You said you would do better
Better hasn't come
Silently waiting
Blame it on the alcohol
Blocking your brain
Tired of excuses
We
      Are
            Silently
                      Waiting

Epilogue

Black Gardenias is more than pain, sadness and complaints rather *Black Gardenias* is stories about love---love of self, family, women, community and God. We are all called individually to live full lives, whole and productive in the face of challenges. The ability to move around, between, over and under the messy stuff that can cripple us is a testimony that this book seeks to provide in some small way to you, the reader.

Justice, redemption, grace and mercy are codifying jewels of agency in the lives you have read about. They are visible in the words of cleaning women and market women. They are behind pale blue shades, in abortion clinics, in fields covered with wildflowers, crowded classrooms, nail salons and nursing homes. We can find these jewels of agency lying on futons, at church with our purple felt hats sisters and even while jumping rope. Agency resides in our imagination constantly defining and redefining who we are in the midst of pain. I can only hope you found this reservoir of love woven throughout these stories, verses and poems.

Black Gardenias reminds us that love in not easy, it's not always obvious and sometimes it is presumed absent, like brothers wearing hoodies and eating skittles in the night. But this transformative radical love that moves from the inside out, gathered from a place of deep self-exploration is necessary if we are to reach the Promised Land and if we are to live authentically, free and whole.

Made in the USA
Charleston, SC
22 March 2014